DEALING

tarot poems and pictures

poems by david wasserman
art by helen castillo

DEALING

tarot poems and pictures

poems by david wasserman
art by helen castillo

+ for katie -

+ para mi vida, migdalia -

i stayed up all night playing poker with tarot cards
i got a full house and four people died
—steven wright

⊙ CONTENTS ⊙

I MAJOR ARCANA I

the fool +

dealing
with these sorceries
cut off from your hand

the fool -

in waiting
i'm wasting
a way without you

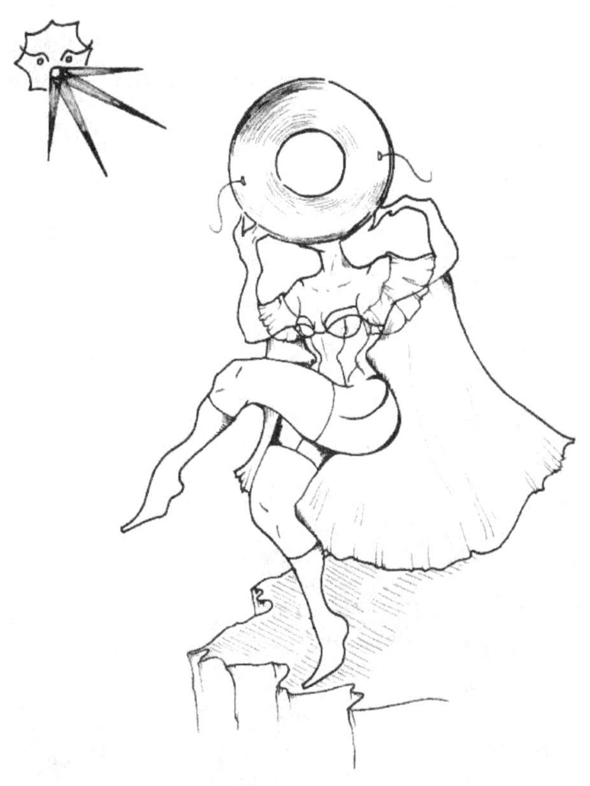

the magician +

experienced now
i escaped
your eternity
my pledge turn prestige

the magician -

magic can't make
these thorns
stop stinging

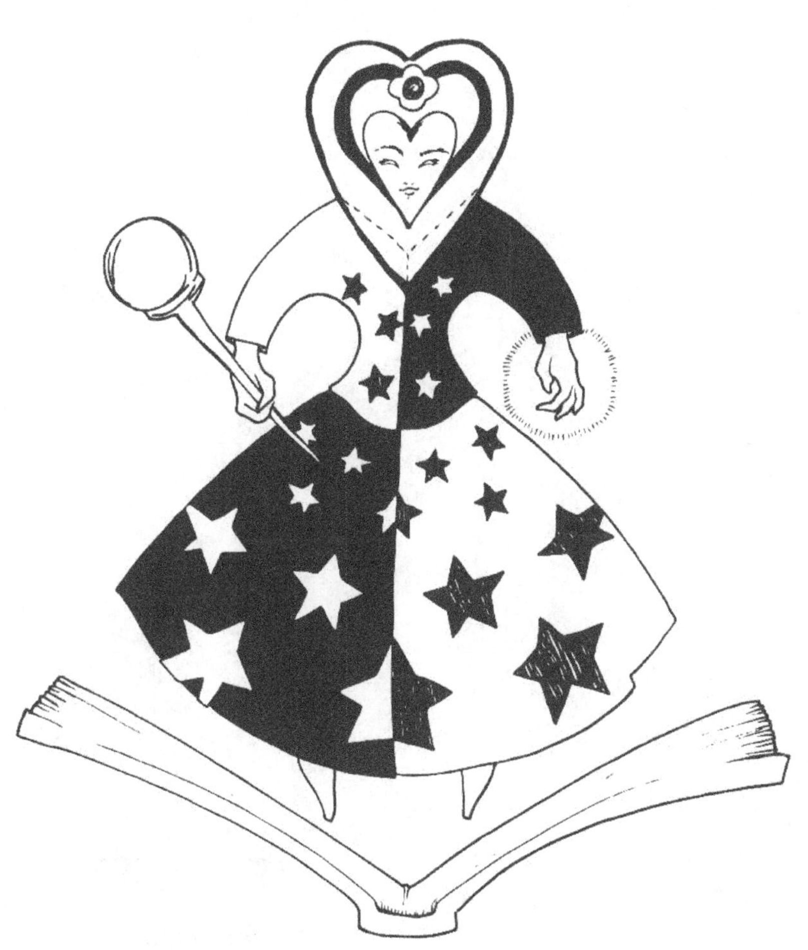

the high priestess +

i trust myself
and refuse
to return

the high priestess -

your cold moon
burns in my brain
i can't stop dreaming you

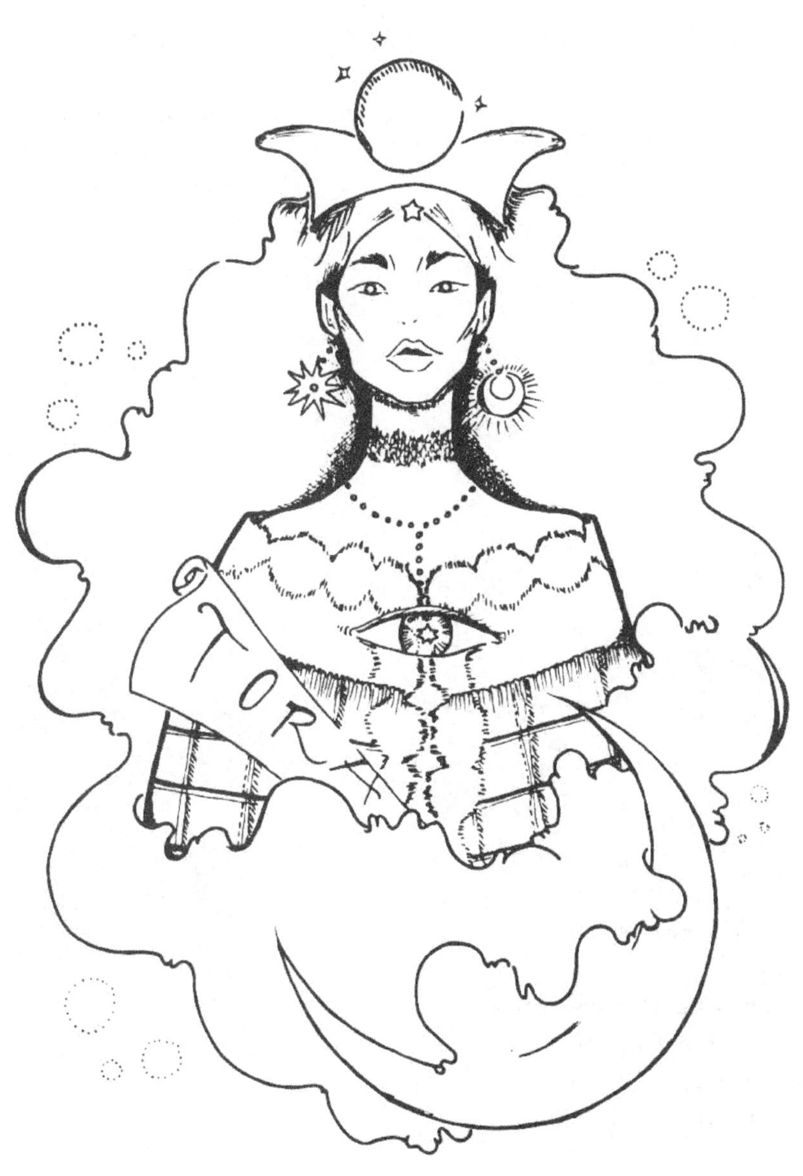
TORA

the empress +

worthy worthy worthy
i create
my own pleasure

the empress -

my bottled message
meant for you
always for you
hidden from you

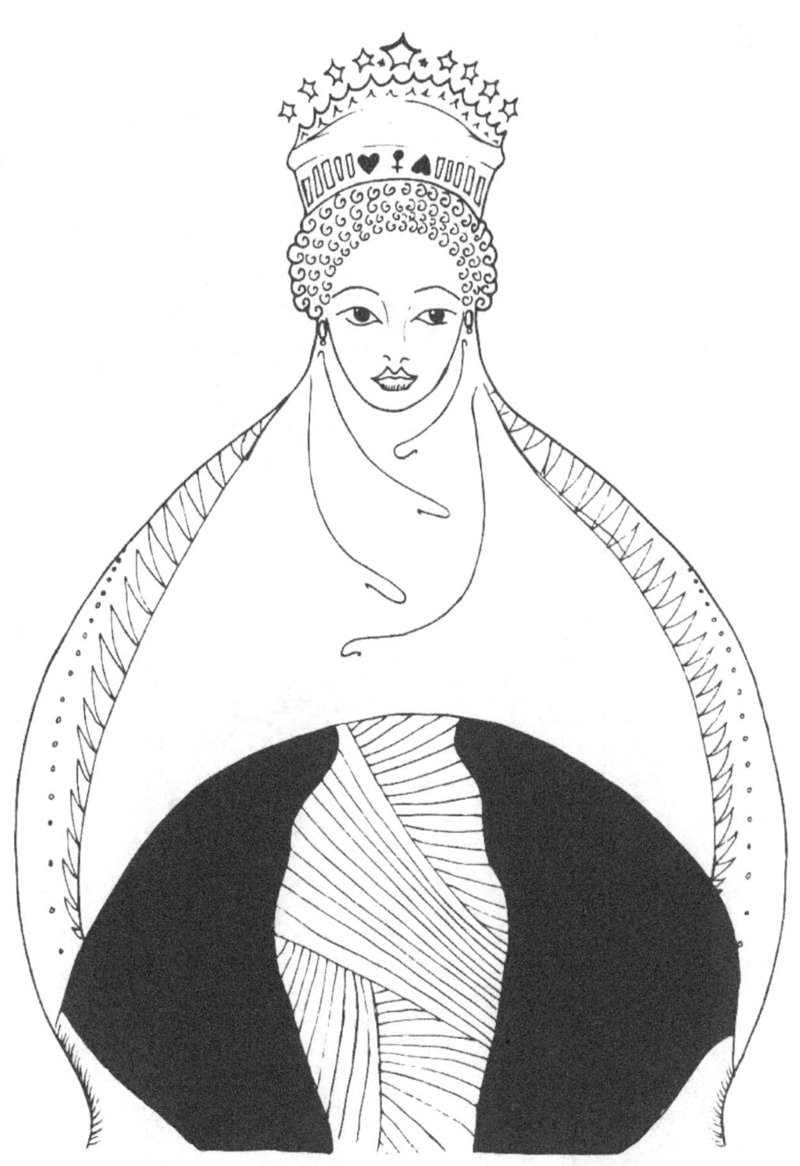

the emperor +

my wounds
were battle scars
all along

the emperor -

i feign to feel
less
powerless

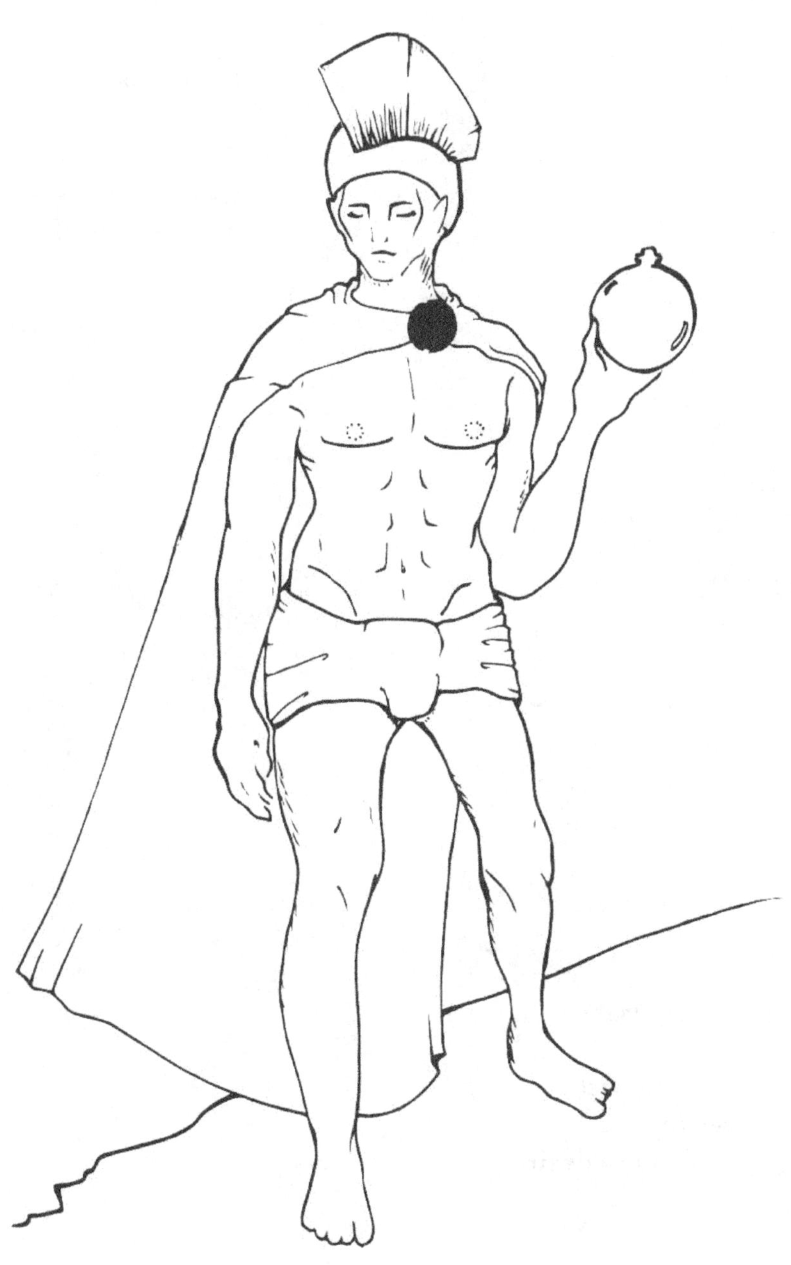

the hierophant +

i believe
as you believe
in myself

the hierophant -

your iron fist
fires my ire
yet also my desire

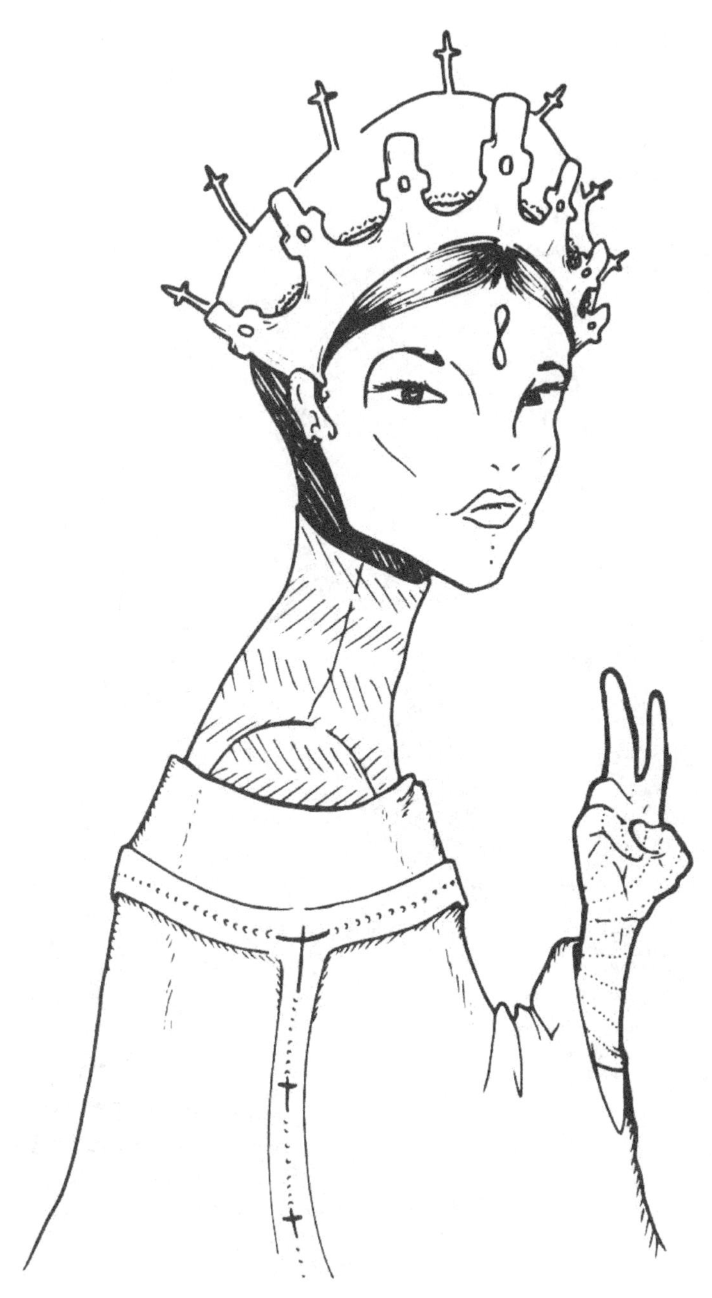

the lovers +

nothing to hide
and everything to seek
i choose choices

the lovers -

all this air
fleshing between
my mountain
your lake

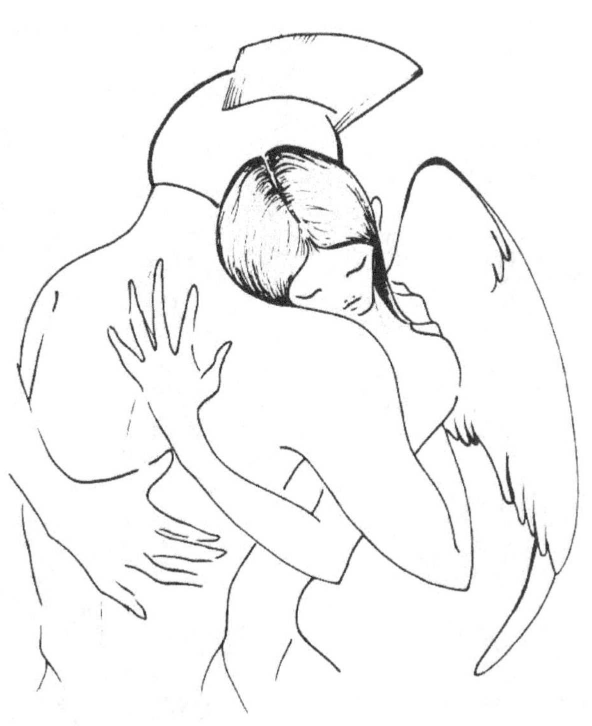

the chariot +

balanced
arched back asking
and boldly basking
amongst stars and sky

the chariot -

black and white before
me
a city upside down
you
rain rein reign

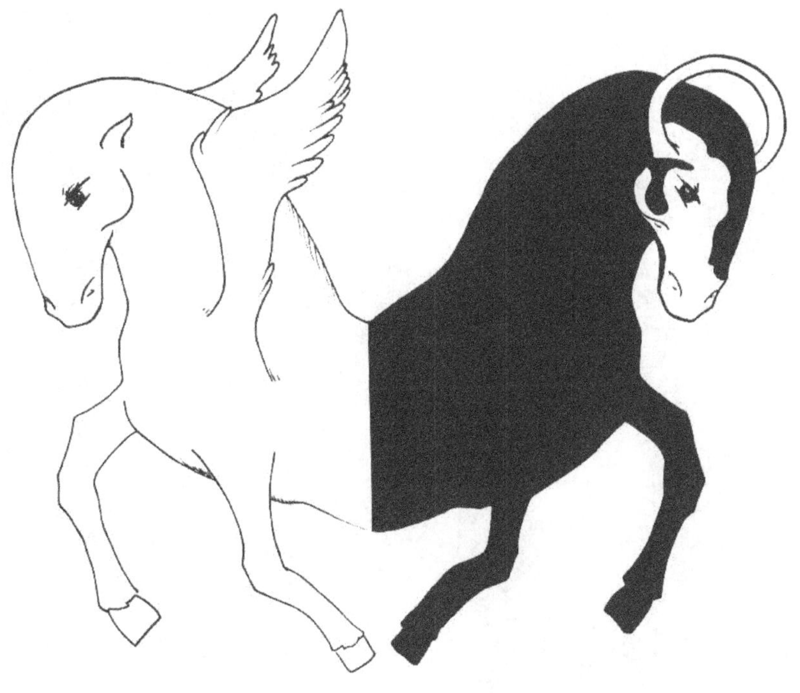

strength +

a lemon sky
breaks between
leminscate
and
lion

strength -

despairing and deceived
trapped inside my stone pillar
doubting forever

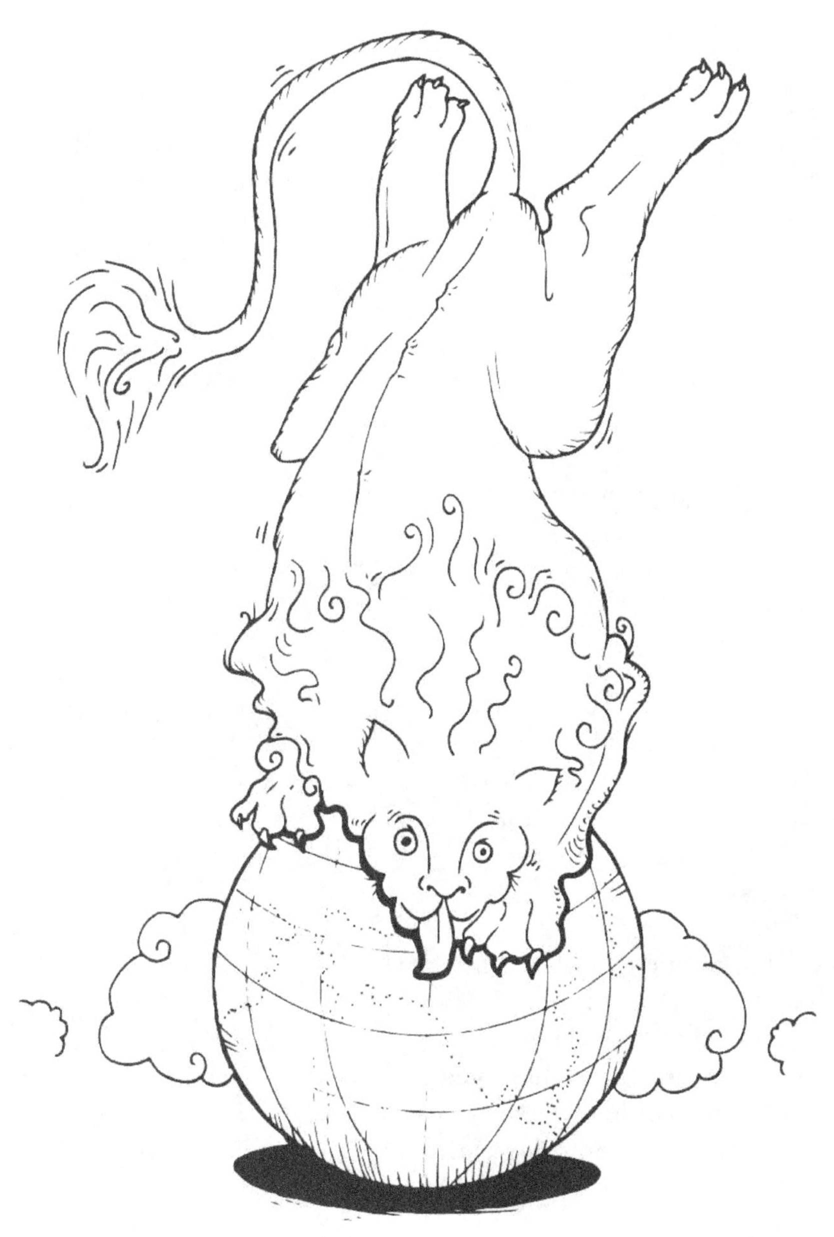

the hermit +

i searched
my snow shrouded soul
lantern lit it led
me to you

the hermit -

stared at by snowy
pearls that were her eyes
i'm invisible
waiting in your wasteland

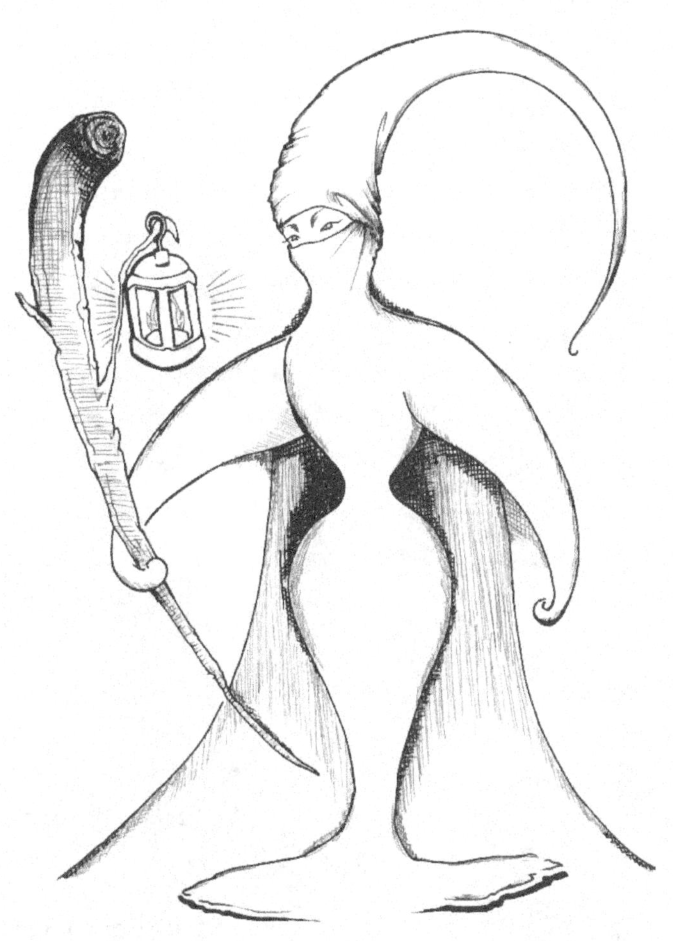

wheel of fortune +

it doesn't matter
where on a wheel
we fall
when wearing wings

wheel of fortune -

spinning
without wisdom
riddled with
your name

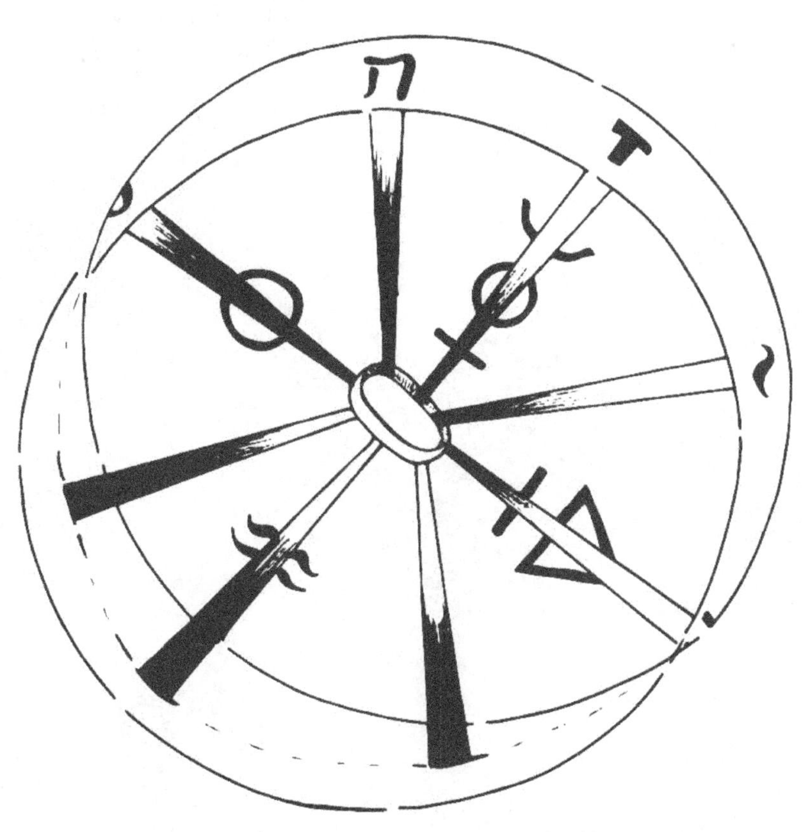

justice +

clasp your cloak
and sword
it's time to serve
what i deserve

justice -

coldly cloaked in red
gold gone
cut off
from your left hand

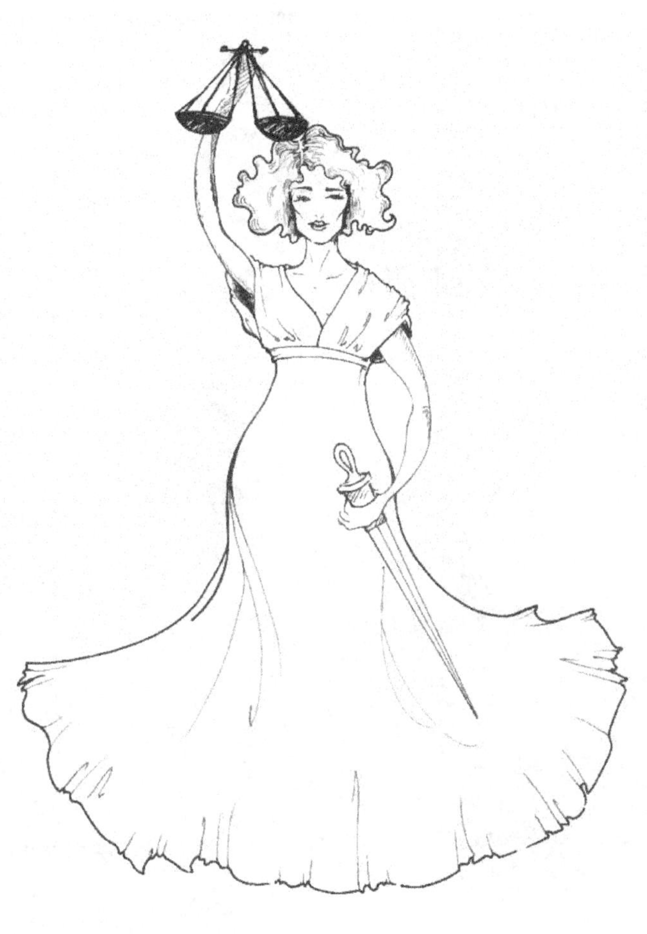

the hanged man +

suspend your
disbelief
and shed your
light on me

the hanged man -

i am worth
more than your
fifty-thousand
pieces of silver

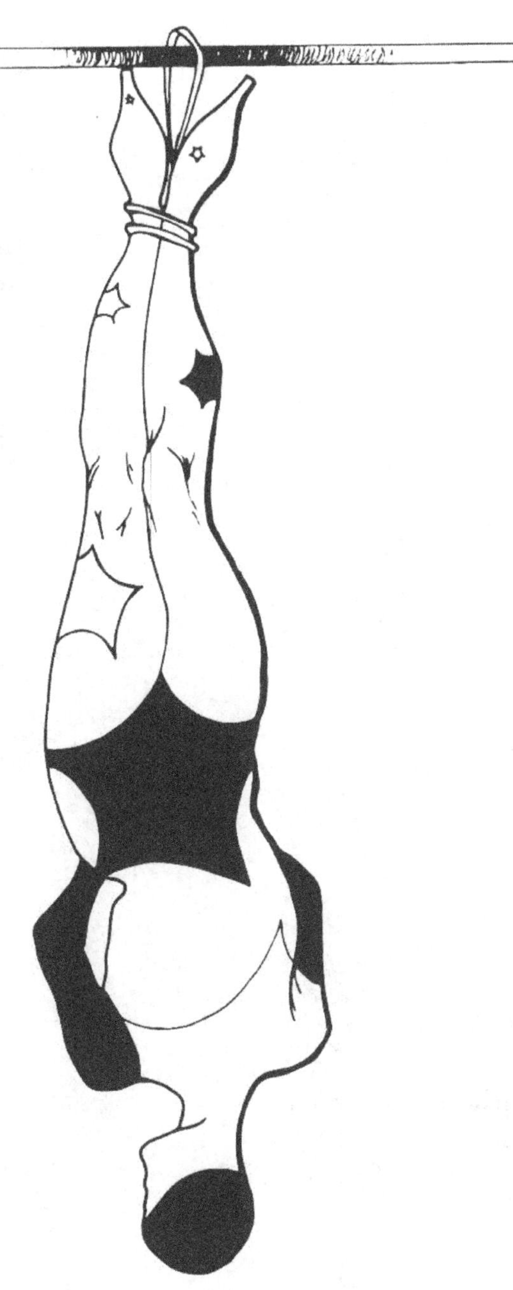

death +

you died with me
we rose from
fire and sulfur
screaming across the sky

death -

without you i died
a second death
the two and then the one

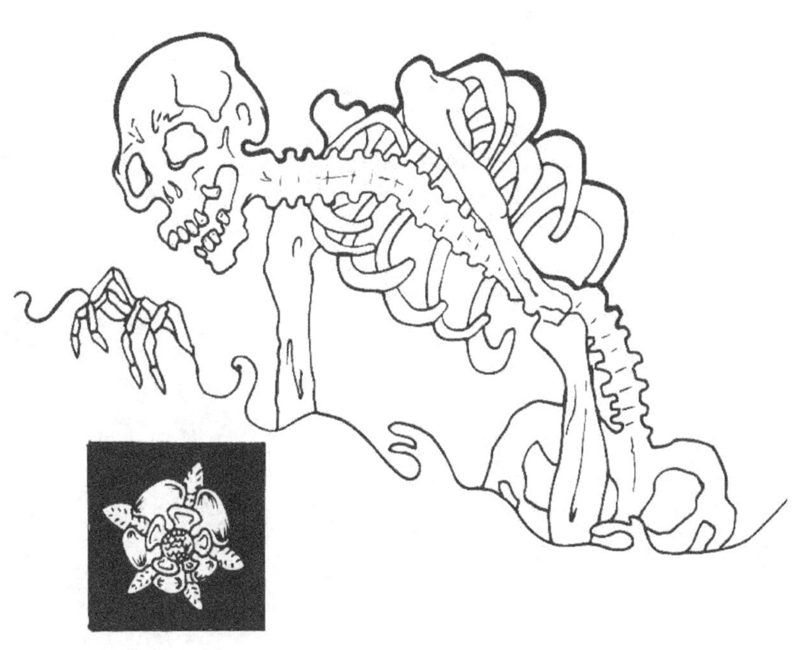

temperance +

somewhere between
wine and water
at peace with my art
at peace with your heart

temperance -

what am i
but diluted dreams
you once desired

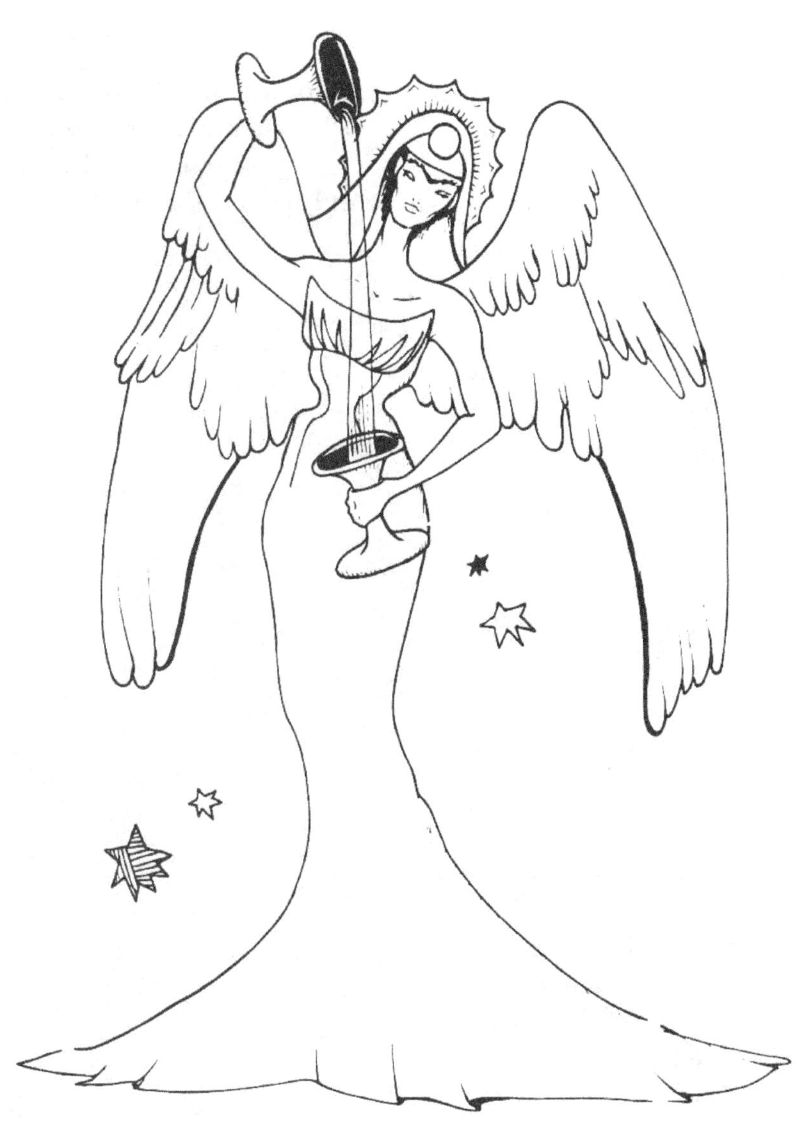

the devil +

changing my chains to
become a perverse
reverse vampire
and spit back some life

the devil -

how is it possible
to be so detached
yet ache for so much
i bleed and burn
below your altar

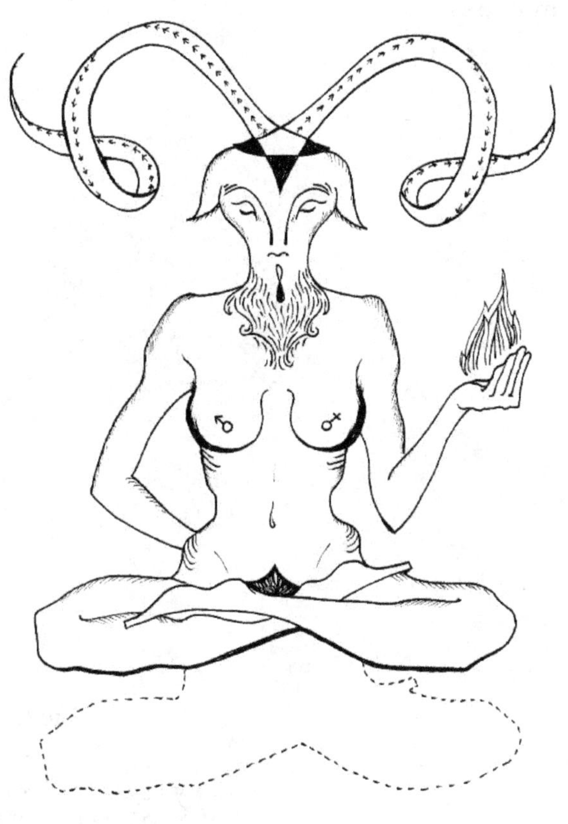

the tower +

i'm breaking apart
he ripped your dress
and my heart
out of my chest

the tower -

you assure me my
flash fire falling
is a necessary
harrowing

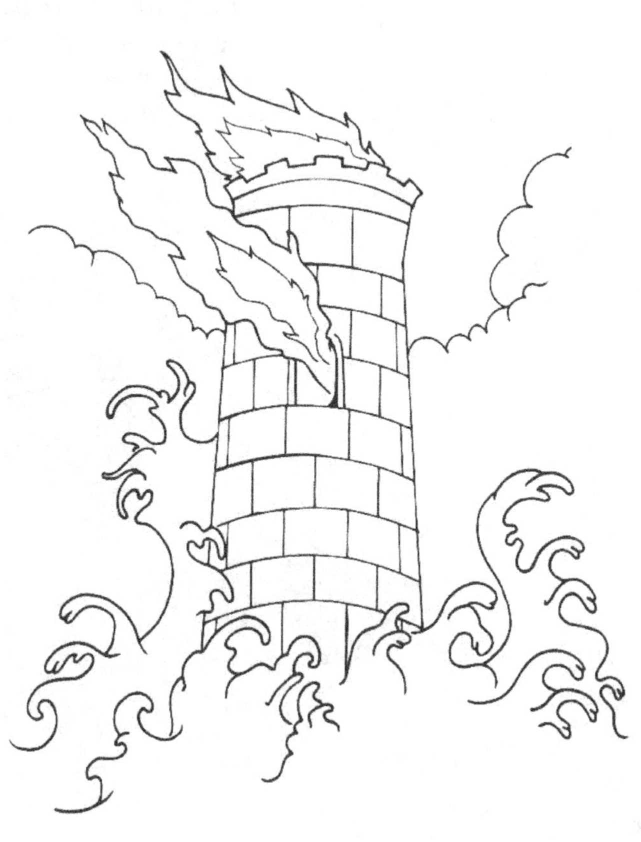

the star +

new faith and trust
no longer in debt
i might forgive but
i will not forget

the star -

when i was little
stars seemed beautiful
but now i know
most are only ghosts

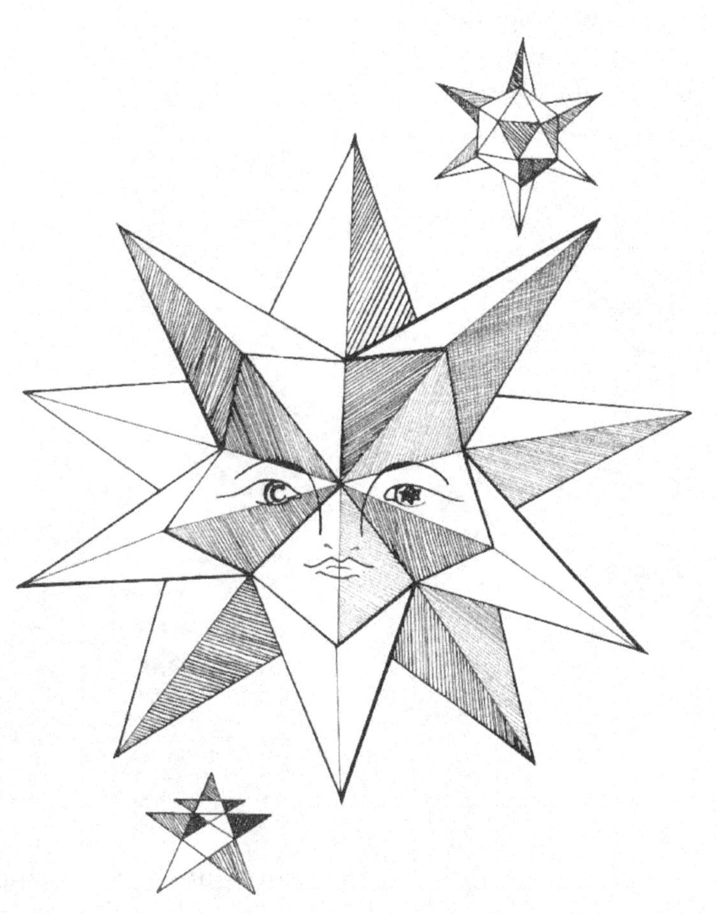

the moon +

most memories
have haunting hues
until you understand
moonlight is merely
sunlight leftovers

the moon -

sunlight slowly slicing
through though
you still have
your shadows

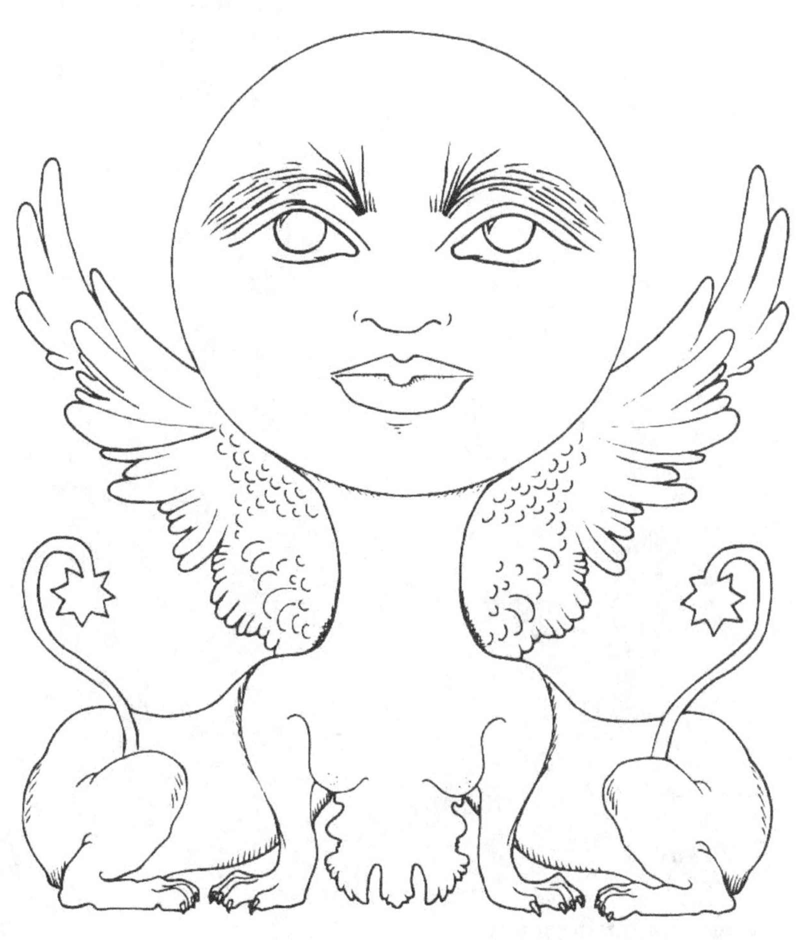

the sun +

rays radiating
from fresh flowers
flags and
flesh

the sun -

does my smile seem
as empty to you
as it feels to me

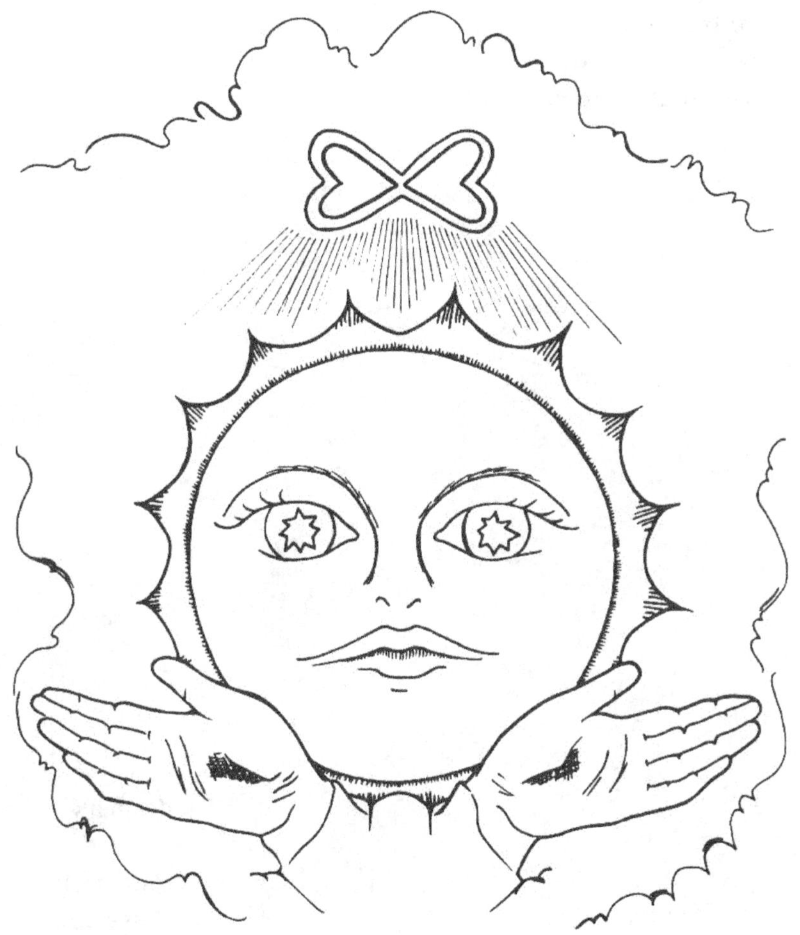

judgement +

the gypsy witch said
to let go of
the sleeping dead
and reach the river's end

judgement -

i might make it through
if i could see the
puppets dallying

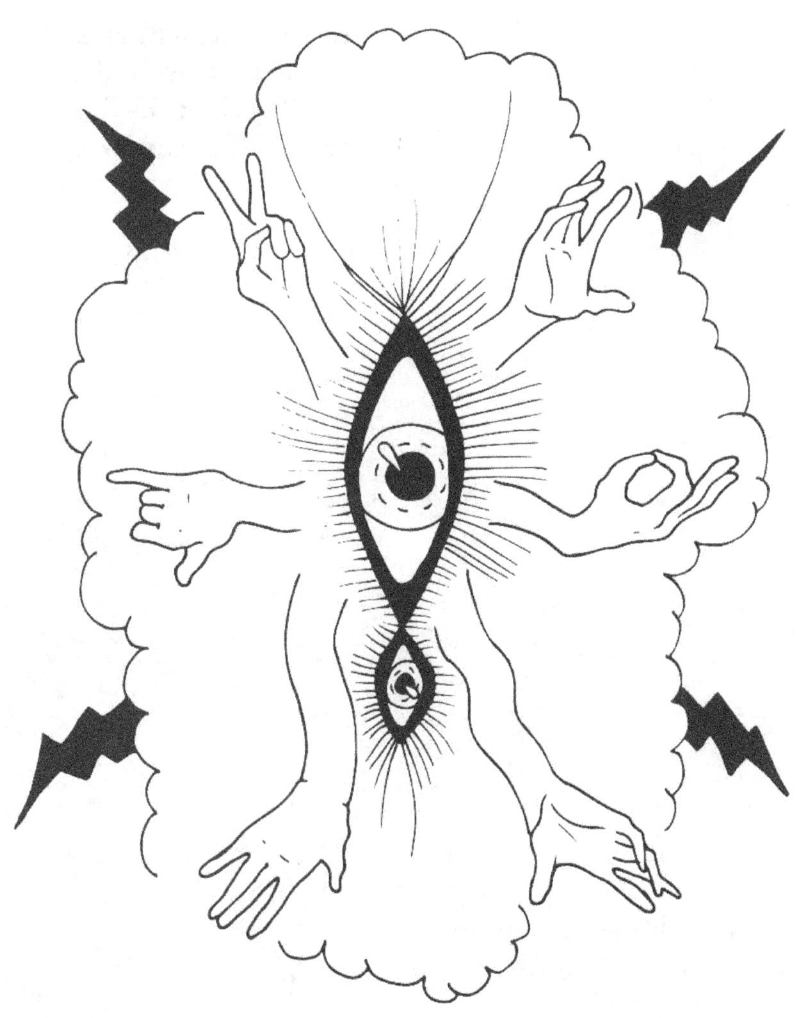

the world +

a rose and its whiteness
fooled fortune tellers
i'll ask of the dead
on behalf of the living

the world -

those things left unsaid
chirped and muttered
finding me forever
tied inside your world

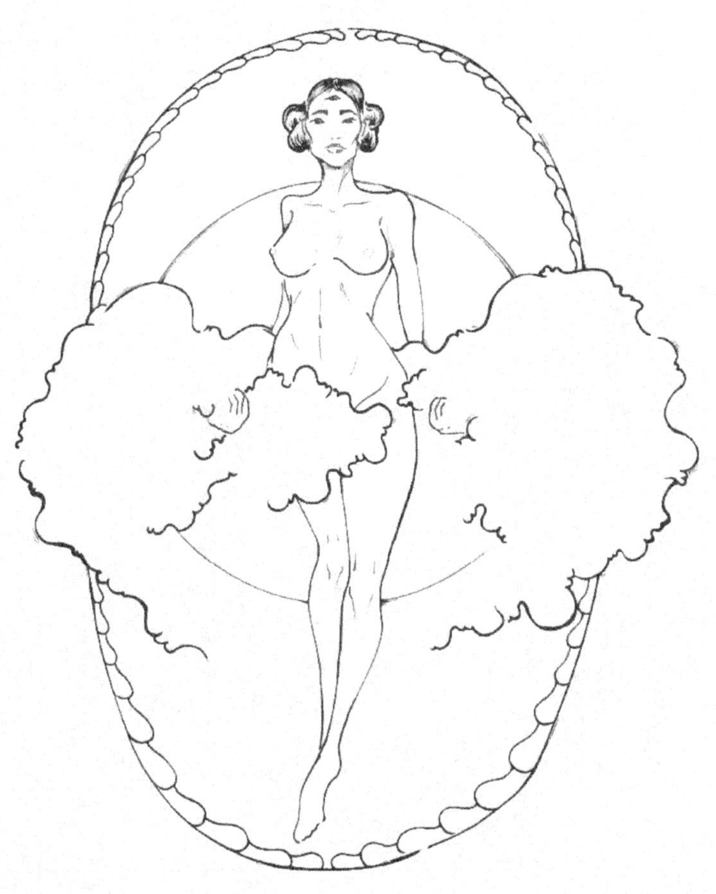

II WANDS II

ace of wands

beginnings
finished the fortune teller
are already
evaporating

II wands II

two paths before me
your ocean
his cliff
will waves or wind
batter my body

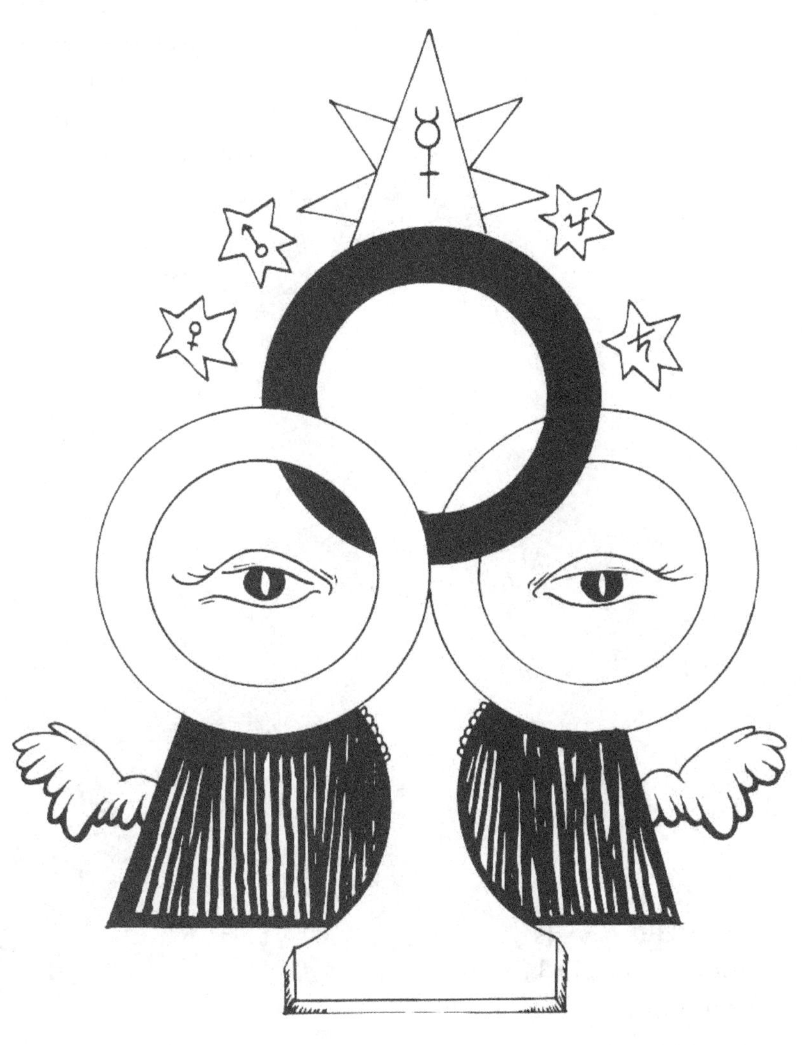

III wands III

so focused on the
falling
stop
see the horizon

IV wands IV

balanced by
your four wands
your firm foundation
you put down your arms
and held me

V wands V

what are we now but
clockworks of orange
wound up and wild
whacking at the wind

VI wands VI

dust off your secret
spineless butcher's broom
resting on the shelf
and come out

VII wands *VII*

i worked too hard to be
together
to allow this dark lady
to get her

VIII wands *VIII*

flowing freely
hurdling over
hurtling past
past hurting

IX wands IX

barriers i've built
but i will break through
for you

X wands X

ten wands
watch
my melted
heart

page of wands

don't forget to dream
said the salamander

knight of wands

fueled by fire
i am left leaning
lustful
and no longer
wandering
back to you

queen of wands

those sunflower sprouts
foolishly followed
your sunny disguise
but i've seen that black cat
stalking around you

king of wands

a flame
i used to be one of
the tongues of fire
licking their way up
your feet to your legs
to my sky
you used to own

III CUPS III

ace of cups

i dove in and drowned
myself in your love
i bathed all my senses
in you

II cups II

this tension
snake rings
rippling out from
my cup to yours

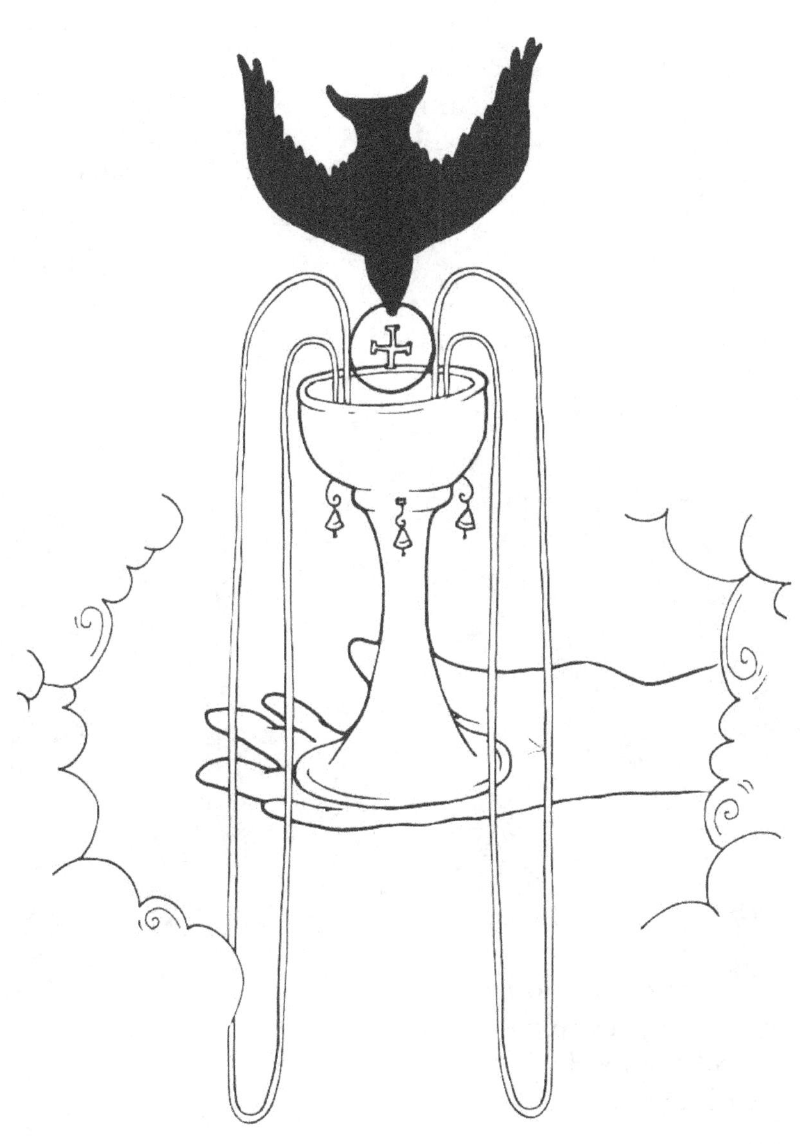

III cups III

our table for two
now set forever
with three glasses

IV cups IV

have another another
to clear your cloudy
head and head
back to me

V cups V

i spilled my secrets
and lost everything
returning to you

VI cups VI

yellowing over time
good memories
past disappointments

VII cups VII

shadowed by seven
demons you left
smoking and soaking
in our deadly sins

VIII cups VIII

my misery
and pleasure
waxing and waning
within your valley

IX cups IX

my blue background gone
i was so convinced
you would get better

X cups X

i wish nothing more
than to drink from these
cups filled from rainbows

page of cups

the gentle pisces
turned a page and
possibilities
bloomed around her

knight of cups

your dreams are waiting
for you to wake up

queen of cups

your mother made your
milk and my madness
flow from her

king of cups

there is a bottle
filled with frozen tears
burning between us
but this simmering
could thaw that coldness

IV SWORDS IV

ace of swords

the psychic said
a sword can be
words used sharply

II swords II

your moonlight glinting
hinting at something
more
a new one sky view

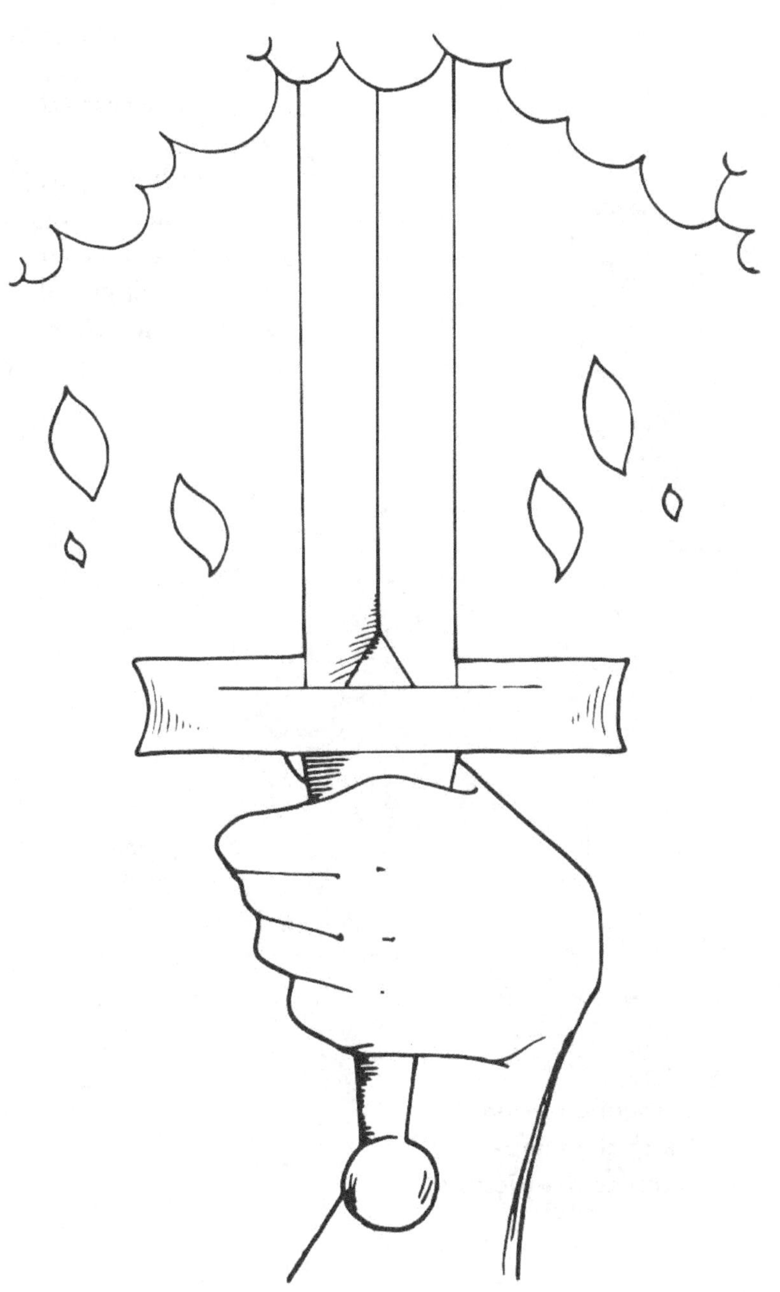

III swords III

at home just
delivering
daggers to each other
what happened
i used to love you

IV swords IV

i wait
for someone to take
a look at the frame
as much as the picture

V swords V

a once little prince
hit with the venom
of growing up
and wanting more

VI swords VI

your swamp of despair
submerged my heavy
head and eyelids in
tears screaming silent
bubbles thinking you
might miss my salty
water when i leave

VII swords VII

stealing seven swords
or stars or secrets
only invites cuts
or burns or regrets

VIII swords VIII

three wise monkeys
and eight sharp swords
so blind to the thousand
slow slicings you deliver
me at every turn

IX swords IX

there's a clock in your bedroom
with the battery missing
you didn't like how it sounded
or how it kept you up at night
a lord of cruelty
with your thoughts

X swords X

i sailed toward your stars
in the southern sky
searching for something
rich and strange but you
stabbed all my sailors
the dark and the light

page of swords

i heard a door close
when i was born
old flames are always
hardest to extinguish
hardest to keep burning

knight of swords

butterflies and birds
push back against your wind
when does my breath become mine

queen of swords

here are mother's hand and sword
look through the glass to see her
clouds of clarity
still have hints of sorrow

king of swords

i gave you love
you gave me facts
because what are we
really
but bones bumping into one another

V PENTACLES V

ace of pentacles

starting today let's
dust off those places
others will never know and
you and i forgot

II pentacles II

done riding the waves
i won't watch all your
struggles to juggle
now and forever

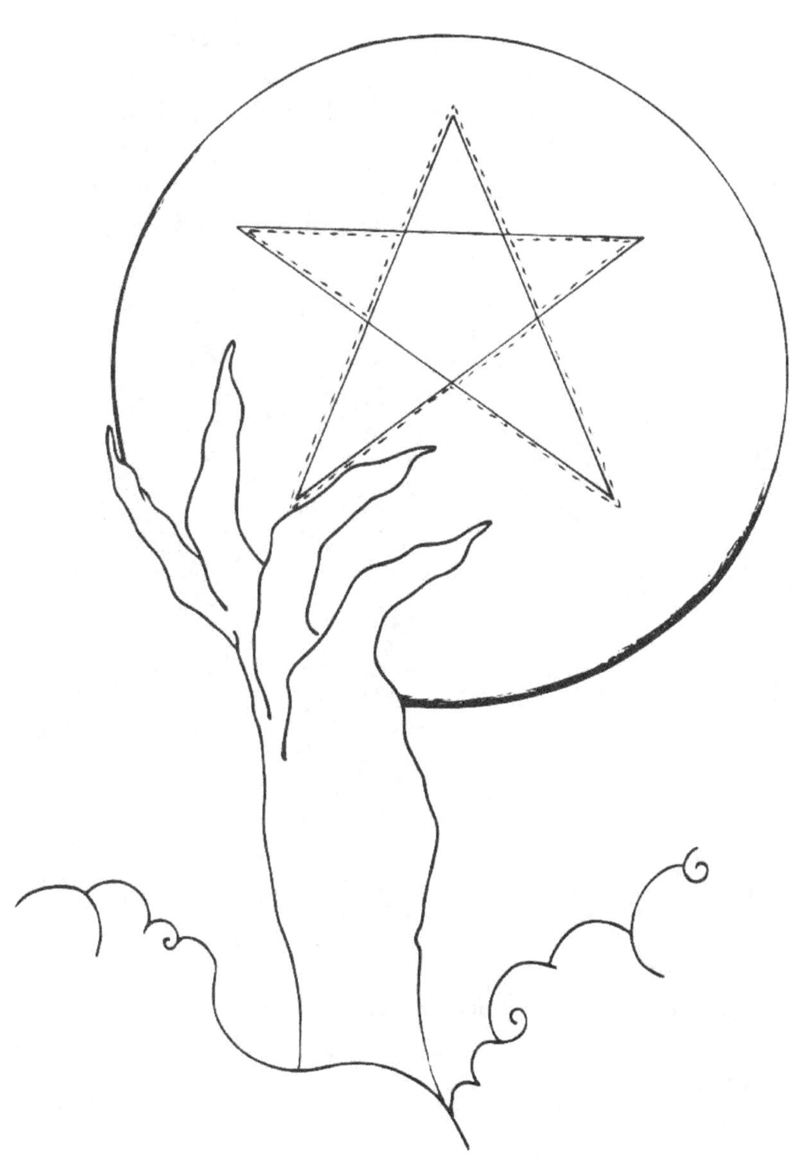

III pentacles III

lost among the cards
you the opposite of me
let's find each other
transformed to tigers

IV pentacles IV

i met a man
consumed with counting stars
i held onto you
a vain violet
i would never leave

V pentacles V

we let the baby
cry too long and wolves
showed up at our door
his haunted house
holds on to one too
many memories

VI pentacles VI

can i catch this
kindness falling from
your unreal city
to make my heart less
grey bleak and greedy

VII pentacles VII

time has killed a bit
of the sweetness
the pleasure was yours
but the sweat was mine

VIII pentacles VIII

this ring
a promise
of work as much as love
let your armor rest
and let me hold you free

IX pentacles IX

you sure took your time
girl who saw a thing
in a forest
her red hood hides her
hawkish intents

X pentacles X

you saw the music
as light without end
but i am tethered
to every single
one of your heartbeats

page of pentacles

brilliantly sunny
as if passing through
your atmosphere
to burn you brighter

knight of pentacles

love did not crack
like a geode for me
one small tap and
feelings crystalized
my love for you
had to be tamed
and taught to behave

queen of pentacles

a skillful teacher
softening here
hardening there
rabbits rarely freeze
in front of your faith

king of pentacles

i want to be more
than the dripping
in your dark basement
i gave you my
flesh with the blood in it

ABOUT THE AUTHOR

David Wasserman is an elementary school teacher and lives in the mostly quiet woods of Connecticut with his wife and daughter. He would be most likely to turn over the Knight of Cups.

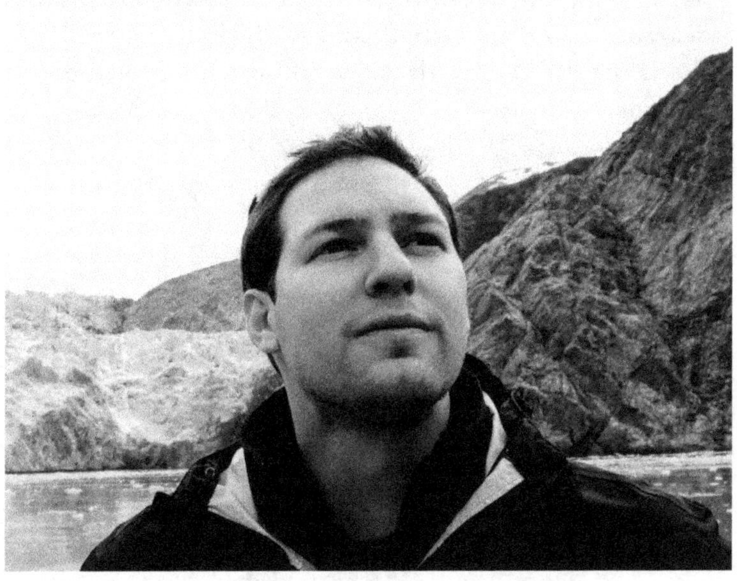

More information can be found at
www.davidwassermanbooks.com

ABOUT THE ARTIST

Helen Castillo was born and raised with pen, ink, paintbrush, and sewing needle in hand. Her biggest inspiration is her mother's compassion and ability to trek through all difficulties with poise and grace. After three consecutive seasons of Project Runway, her dreams of becoming a world-renowned fashion designer have flourished, and with that, the card she is most likely to draw would be the Queen of Wands.

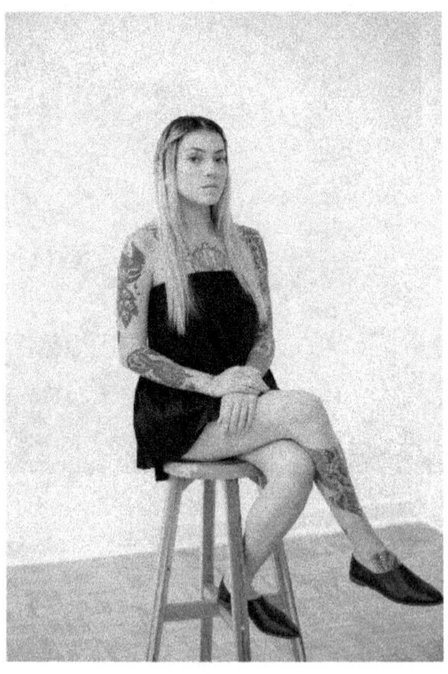